CHARLIE BROWN'S 'CYCLOPEDIA

Super Questions and Answers and Amazing Facts

Featuring Cars and Trains and Other Things that Move

Volume 4

Based on the Charles M. Schulz Characters

Funk & Wagnalls, Inc.

Photograph and Illustration Credits: Bryan and Cherry Alexander/Bruce Coleman, Inc., 147; American Museum of Natural History, 148; American Trucking Associations, Inc., 184, 185; Association of American Railroads, 174, 175, ix; James J. Cariello, 164; John M. Christensen, 185; Henning Christoph/Black Star, 181; Eleanor Ehrhardt, 180; Giorgio Gualco/Bruce Coleman, Inc., 147; Indianapolis Motor Speedway Corporation, 168; Kennebec Valley Chamber of Commerce/Paul Fournier, 190; Larry Lee/The Image Bank, x; The Metropolitan Museum of Art, Rogers Fund, 1903, 150; National Aeronautics and Space Administration, 169; National Automotive History Collection, Detroit Public Library, 162, 164; Newell and Adlington/American Museum of Natural History, 147; New York City Fire Department Photo Unit, 186, 187; New York State Department of Commerce, 147, 172, 191; San Francisco Visitors Bureau, 171; Shor/American Museum of Natural History, 147; Kenneth W. Stauffer, 161.

A large part of the material in this volume was previously published in *Charlie Brown's Third Super Book of Questions and Answers.*

Introduction

Welcome to volume 4 of *Charlie Brown's 'Cyclopedia!* Have you ever wondered how Roman emperors traveled, or who invented the bicycle, or what a horseless carriage is? Charlie Brown and the rest of the *Peanuts* gang are here to help you find the answers to these questions and many more about cars and trains and other things that move. Have fun!

Charlie Brown on Land

How did people first travel?

They walked. Before people knew of any other way to travel, they used what nature gave them to move from one place to another—their feet. But foot travel was slow. When people wanted to go long distances, they had to spend weeks, months, or even years.

Why did people use animals for travel?

Large animals such as mules and camels are strong enough to carry people on their backs. And they don't tire as quickly as people. So when men, women, and children started to ride animals, they were able to travel long distances more quickly than before. They were also able to get to where they were going without becoming so tired.

How did people first carry things?

People first carried things in their arms and on their backs—and they still do. They also balance things on their heads. But arms, backs, and heads can carry only lightweight loads. People quickly tire from their burdens. So about 8,000 years ago, they began to tame animals to carry things.

What animals have people used to carry things?

People have used whatever strong, easy-to-tame animals they have found living in their lands. And they still use these "beasts of burden" for carrying things and for pulling carts, wagons, and sleds. In the desert lands of Egypt and Syria people use oxen, donkeys, and camels. Camels are especially good for desert travel. Deserts are dry. Camels can go for long periods without water. Reindeer are ideal for the people of icy Lapland. Reindeer move quickly in snow and can carry up to 300 pounds. Llamas are good mountain climbers. They carry things for the Indians of Peru in the Andes Mountains. The people of ancient Iran were the first to tame horses. Horses can move faster for a longer period of time than all other animals. In India elephants carry loads on their backs and even in their trunks. Eskimos near the North Pole train dogs to pull sleds and carry light loads.

Reindeer

Indian elephant

Camel

Donkey

Dog sled team

Llamas

What did the American Indians use to carry supplies?

Many American Indians used the travois (truh-VOY) to carry things. It was made of two long poles. The front or middle of the poles was attached to an animal. The bottom end dragged along the ground. The Indians strapped their supplies to the poles. For many years they used a dog to pull the travois. But after European settlers brought horses to America, the Indians used a horse instead.

How did Roman emperors travel?

The emperors and the rich people of Rome were carried on litters. A litter is a couch on two poles. Four slaves carried it on their shoulders. While the slaves walked with their load, the passenger lounged on the couch. There were so many litters that they caused real traffic jams in ancient Rome.

Did people ever use sleds without snow?

Yes, they did, and they still do. The sledge was one of the earliest vehicles—objects that carry people or things from one place to another. At first a sledge was just a flat piece of wood, dragged along the ground. Then people added wooden runners to it. These were much like the metal runners on a modern snow sled. Oxen, and possibly other animals, pulled the sledges.

What good were sledges?

Early people found that an object moved along the ground more easily with runners under it than without them. Later, people discovered that wheels made movement even easier. But runners work better than wheels in sand and in marshes. Wheels sink into sand. They get stuck in swamps and marshes. Runners don't. Because of this, people in Lapland still use horse-drawn sledges to carry hay over marshy areas.

149

Who invented the wheel?

No one knows exactly who invented it or when. But we do know that people were using it about 5,000 years ago. These people lived in the areas now known as Iraq, Syria, and Turkey. The first wheels were probably round slices of a log.

The idea for the wheel probably came from log "rollers." People used to place logs under a large object. They would then roll the object across the logs. But there was a problem with this method. As soon as the object passed over a log, the log had to be carried to the front of the object again.

Without the wheel we would have no cars, trains, airplanes, watches, clocks, movie projectors, or washing machines!

What was the first vehicle with wheels?

The chariot may have been the first wheeled vehicle. It was a two-wheeled cart, open at the back. At first, a chariot was pulled by donkeys. Then horses replaced the donkeys. People who rode in chariots did not sit in them—they stood. Many ancient peoples—the Greeks and the Romans, for example—used them when fighting wars. Sometimes a soldier would stand in the chariot with the horse's reins tied to his waist. Then his hands were free to hold a spear and to fight.

Around the same time that the chariot was invented, other vehicles were developed. Four-wheeled wagons and many styles of two-wheeled carts were used for carrying loads.

Etruscan chariot

When did people start using carriages?

About 2,000 years ago ancient Romans were using carriages—horse-drawn vehicles for carrying seated people. But carriages were most popular in Europe and America in the 1700s. They remained popular through the 1800s. During that time carriages were lightweight, fast, and graceful.

Rockaway

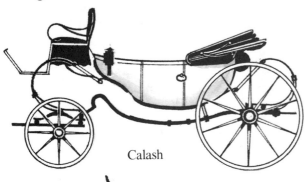
Calash

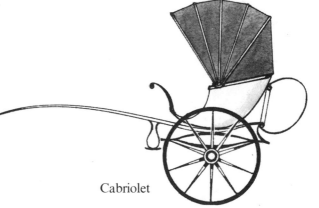
Cabriolet

Buggy

What were some different kinds of carriages?

Here are pictures of a few kinds of carriages. They were all pulled by horses—from one to six, depending on the type of carriage.

151

How did it feel to ride in a cabriolet?

The cabriolet (cab-ree-uh-LAY) must have given a very gentle, bouncy ride. It was a lightweight carriage. But it had heavy-duty springs under the seat. When a trotting horse pulled the cabriolet over the unpaved roads of the 1800s, the carriage leaped in rhythm.

The French word "cabriolet" means little leap. It comes from an older French word for baby goat. Riding in a cabriolet probably reminded someone of riding on the back of a playful baby goat.

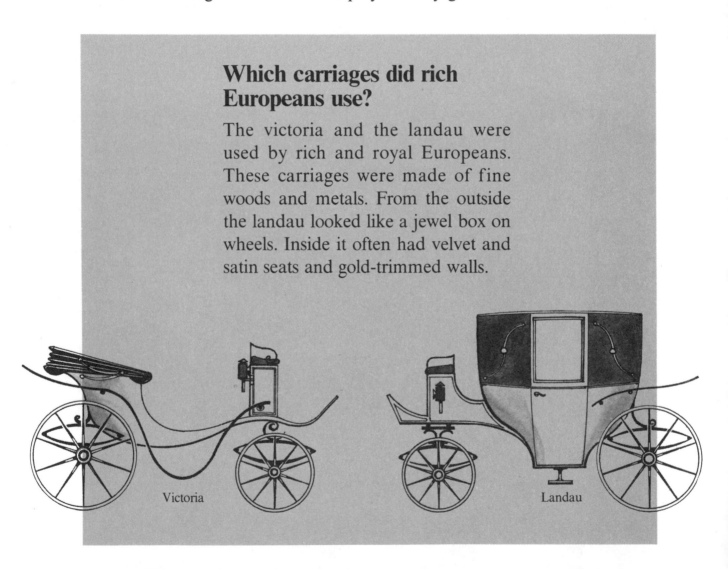

Which carriages did rich Europeans use?

The victoria and the landau were used by rich and royal Europeans. These carriages were made of fine woods and metals. From the outside the landau looked like a jewel box on wheels. Inside it often had velvet and satin seats and gold-trimmed walls.

Victoria

Landau

What was a coach?

Do you remember Cinderella? She rode in a coach when she went to the ball. A coach was a large, four-wheeled carriage. It was closed on the sides and on top. After the 1500s coaches were used in Europe for public transportation. Rich people owned their own private ones. However, their rides were no more comfortable than those of other people. Early roads were very bumpy. Springs were not put under carriage seats until the late 1700s. So, for the first 200 years, even a king had a rough ride!

What was a stagecoach?

A stagecoach was a coach that carried passengers, mail, and sometimes large packages. The inside of the coach seated from four to eight people. The mail, packages, and luggage were placed on the roof, on special racks.

Stagecoaches traveled on regular routes between two or more cities. The drivers changed horses at set stops, or "stages," along the routes. That's how stagecoaches got their name.

These vehicles became popular in Europe in the late 1600s and in America in the late 1700s. After 1825 stagecoaches were slowly replaced by railroads.

What sort of vehicles did American pioneers use to travel west?

American pioneers traveled west in covered wagons pulled by teams of horses. True to its name, a covered wagon was covered by a high, curved canvas top. Pioneer families took their household belongings with them in these sturdy wagons. Usually groups of families traveled together. Their wagons would follow a trail, one behind the other. The long line of wagons was called a wagon train.

Have people ever pulled carts?

Yes. Starting in 1870, men in Japan, China, and some other Asian countries pulled carts that were used as taxicabs. The carts were called rickshas, or jinrickishas (jin-RICK-shaws). A man stood at the front between two poles attached to the ricksha. He held the two poles and ran. In this way, he often pulled passengers 20 to 30 miles a day.

In most Asian countries rickshas have been outlawed. Pedicabs have replaced them. A pedicab is a three-wheeled cart. It has two wheels in the front with a passenger cart over them. The back looks like the back half of a bicycle. A driver sits on it and pedals.

Who invented the bicycle?

A Frenchman, Comte Mède de Sivrac (cawnt med duh see-VROCK), built an early wooden model in 1790. It had no pedals and no steering bar. A rider had to move and steer by putting his feet on the ground and pushing. De Sivrac's bicycle should have been called a "walking machine."

In about 1816 a German, Baron Karl von Drais, built a model with a steering bar. And in 1839 foot pedals were finally added by a Scottish blacksmith named Kirkpatrick Macmillan. This bicycle was much more like the ones we see today.

An early bicycle called a penny-farthing had a front wheel about nine times larger than the back wheel!

156

How does a bicycle work?

Between the two large wheels of a bicycle is a much smaller wheel with little teeth on it. This small wheel is called a sprocket. The foot pedals are attached to this sprocket. When a rider pushes the foot pedals, the sprocket turns. One end of a chain fits around the sprocket. The other end fits around a smaller sprocket in the center of the rear wheel of the bicycle. When the large sprocket turns, so does the chain. It turns the small sprocket and the large rear wheel. The bicycle moves forward.

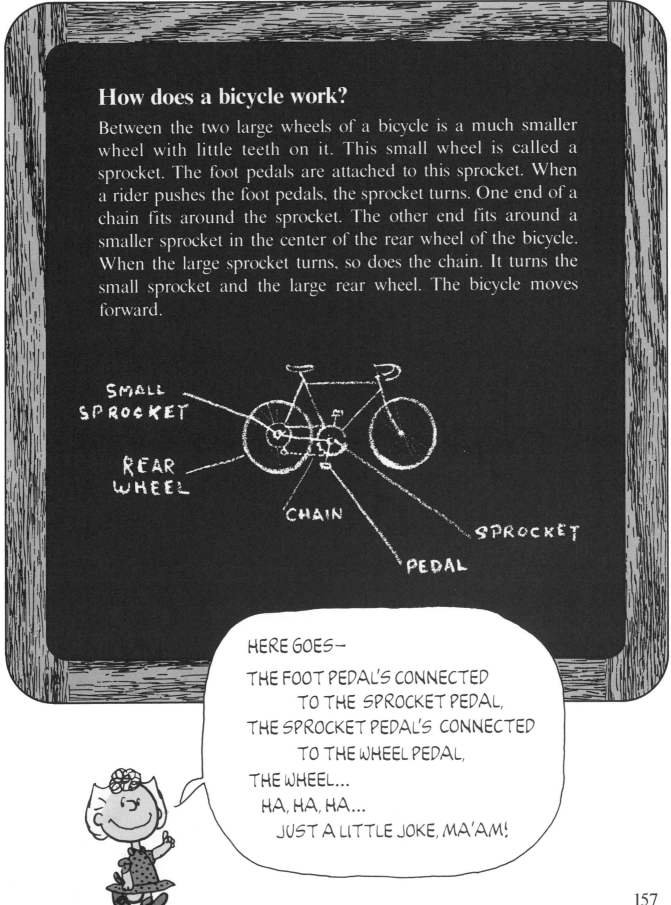

SMALL SPROCKET

REAR WHEEL

CHAIN

SPROCKET

PEDAL

HERE GOES—

THE FOOT PEDAL'S CONNECTED
      TO THE SPROCKET PEDAL,
THE SPROCKET PEDAL'S CONNECTED
      TO THE WHEEL PEDAL,
THE WHEEL...
   HA, HA, HA...
      JUST A LITTLE JOKE, MA'AM!

What was the longest bicycle ever built?

You've probably heard of a bicycle built for two. Well, the longest bicycle was built for 35! It was made in Denmark in 1976. The bike weighed more than a ton and was 72 feet (22 meters) long. That's longer than a dozen regular bicycles placed end to end.

What is the smallest bicycle ever built?

The world's smallest ridable bicycle has wheels just over 2 inches (5 centimeters) high. The bike weighs only two pounds (less than one kilogram). It is so small, it fits in the palm of its builder's hand. Yet he actually rides it at Circus Circus Hotel in Nevada.

How fast can you go on a bicycle?

The average bike rider can cycle up to 12 miles (19 kilometers) an hour. One cyclist reached 140½ miles (225 kilometers) an hour! But he did not go that fast by pedaling alone. He was riding his bicycle right behind a windscreen mounted on a car. The windscreen pushed the air out to the sides so that it did not slow down the movement of the bike and the rider.

Why do people put training wheels on children's bicycles?

If you have learned to ride a bicycle, you know how hard balancing it can be at first. A bicycle tips over when it's standing still. It tips over easily when moving slowly, too. A bike can balance itself only when it is moving very fast. Training wheels help children who haven't learned to pick up speed quickly. The training wheels keep the bike from tipping over until it is moving fast enough to balance itself.

LETS SEE...THAT JUST LEAVES 5 HOURS AND 24 MINUTES MORE TO GO.

One man balanced on a bike for 5 hours and 25 minutes—staying absolutely still!

How do training wheels balance a bicycle?

Training wheels make a bike very hard to tip over. Try this experiment to see why: Stand up straight with your feet close together. Ask someone—someone trustworthy!—to give you a gentle push sideways. With your feet close together, it is easy to fall over. You probably have to take a step to keep from falling. Now stand with your feet about as far apart as your shoulders. Ask your trustworthy person to give you another gentle push—just as hard as before. This time it is much easier to keep from falling over. With your feet farther apart, you are more stable because you have a wider base. The bicycle is the same. Without training wheels, it tips over easily. But when you attach training wheels to it, you make its base much wider. You would have to push the bicycle quite hard to make it fall onto its side.

Why do small children ride on tricycles?

Just as a bicycle with training wheels is hard to tip over, so is a three-wheeled tricycle. When small children ride tricycles, they don't have to worry about balance. They can just have fun!

159

What is a motorcycle?

A motorcycle is any two-wheeled vehicle powered by a gasoline engine. There are several different kinds. Each kind except for the heaviest has a special name. The heaviest motorcycles are called simply motorcycles. They have no engine cover. You can see the engine between the two wheels.

What's the difference between a motorbike and a motor scooter?

They are both kinds of motorcycles, but they are built differently.

A motorbike is very lightweight. It looks a lot like a bicycle with an engine.

A motor scooter looks more like an electric cart than like a bicycle or an ordinary motorcycle. It is wider and heavier than a motorbike but lighter than a standard motorcycle. Its body is covered by a frame which hides the engine.

What was a horseless carriage?

"Horseless carriage" was the nickname given to the first automobiles. And that's exactly what they were—carriages that moved without being pulled by horses. Instead of horses pulling them, automobiles had their own engines. They practically moved themselves. In fact the word "automobile" means self-moving.

160

How did a steam-powered automobile work?

It had a steam engine that boiled water and turned it to steam. Inside the engine was a piece of metal called a piston. The steam pushed the piston back and forth. The piston turned a metal rod that was connected to the car's wheels. When the rod moved, the wheels moved—and so did the car.

Why didn't steam-driven cars last?

Steam-driven cars were unpopular for several reasons. They were so noisy they frightened both horses and people. These cars dirtied the air with smoke wherever they went. And sometimes even hot coals would shoot out of them.

But that was not all. Stagecoach and railroad line owners did not like the new automobiles. They were afraid that if many people rode in these cars, fewer passengers would ride on their lines. In England stagecoach and railroad owners were able to have laws passed that limited the use of steam-driven cars. For example, one law of 1865 said that a signal man had to walk in front of each car and warn people it was coming!

1910 Stanley Steamer

What is an electric car?

An electric car is an automobile powered by one or more electric motors. This means that the motor gets its power from a battery. The battery must be plugged into a wall socket from time to time to be recharged.

Electric cars were popular in the 1890s and early 1900s. They were clean and quiet. They could move as fast as 20 miles (32 kilometers) an hour. But after an electric car had traveled only about 50 miles (80 kilometers), the battery went dead. Because the battery had to be recharged often, people quickly tired of the electric car. Inventors worked to develop a new kind of engine. And they did—the gasoline engine. Gasoline engines were more powerful than electric ones. They cost less to run and their batteries lasted longer.

Who are the "fathers of the modern automobile"?

Two Germans, Gottlieb Daimler and Karl Benz, are considered the fathers of the modern automobile. In 1885, each man, working separately, developed a new kind of engine. It was the kind of gasoline engine we use in cars today. Daimler put his engine in a motorcycle. Benz put his engine in a three-wheeled automobile.

Benz's three-wheel car

WOW! In 1896, the automobile was so new and strange, it was shown in Barnum and Bailey's Circus!

How does the engine of a modern car work?

When the engine is turned on, gasoline goes to a part of the engine called the carburetor (CAR-buh-ray-tur). There, the gasoline mixes with air. The gas and air mixture goes to the cylinders (SILL-in-durz). A car usually has four, six, or eight cylinders. A cylinder is a hollow container that is shaped much like a tin can. In each cylinder is a piston, a solid piece of metal that moves up and down. A piston moves down to suck in the gasoline and air mixture. Then it moves up again. Just as the piston gets near the top of the cylinder, a spark plug gives off an electric spark. This causes the mixture to explode. The heat of the explosion pushes the piston down again. This happens in one cylinder after another, providing the energy to move the car.

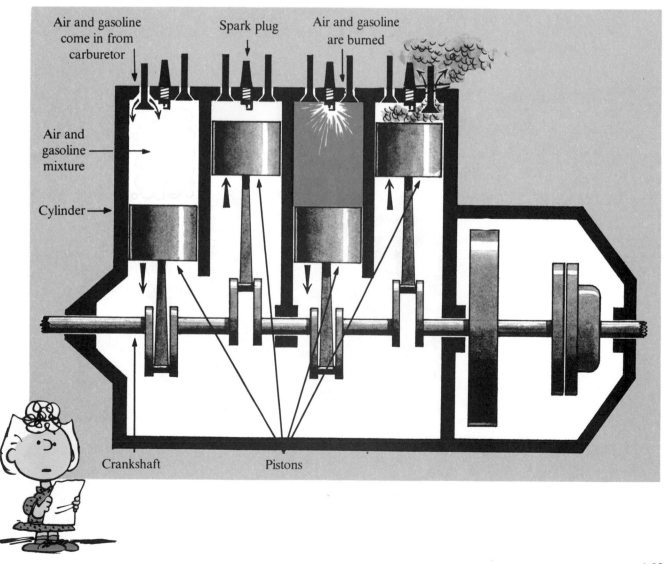

Air and gasoline come in from carburetor

Spark plug

Air and gasoline are burned

Air and gasoline mixture

Cylinder

Crankshaft

Pistons

Who was Henry Ford?

Henry Ford was an American pioneer in building cars. He introduced the moving assembly line. Each worker on an assembly line does just one small job in putting a car together. The parts are on a moving belt. When a worker finishes his or her job, the parts move along to the next worker. Before using Ford's method, workers spent a lot of time doing complicated jobs to make each car. Because of the moving assembly line, factories were able to produce cars more quickly and cheaply than before. Ford could sell his cars for less than other cars, so more people could afford to own them.

By the 1920's a finished Model T Ford came off the assembly line every 10 seconds!

Henry Ford

What was the Model T?

The Model T was Ford's most famous car. The Ford Motor Company built it between 1908 and 1927. To keep the price down, Ford made only small changes in the Model T each year.

THAT'S VERY INTERESTING

One 1936 Ford has been driven more than 1 million 37 thousand miles (1 million 659 thousand kilometers)!

Where does gasoline come from?

Gasoline is made from petroleum. Petroleum is a thick, oily liquid found deep inside the earth. People drill thousands of feet into the ground to get to it. Americans usually call petroleum "oil."

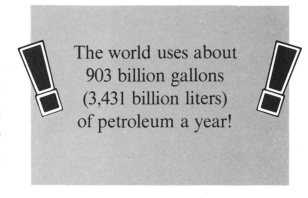

The world uses about 903 billion gallons (3,431 billion liters) of petroleum a year!

What are the dials and knobs on a car's dashboard?

The knobs control the lights, the heater, the windshield wipers, the air conditioner, and the radio. The dials tell a driver how much gas and oil are in the car. They also show how fast the driver is going and if the battery is making or losing electricity.

Why do we put motor oil in our cars?

A car's engine has moving parts. We use motor oil (which is made from petroleum) to keep the engine's parts moving smoothly. The oil provides a thin layer of greasy liquid on the parts. Then they don't get rusty, scrape against each other, or wear out quickly.

Why do cars have license plates?

All states make car owners register their cars. License plates are part of this registration. A license plate can help the police find a stolen car. It can also help identify a car in case of an accident. Finally, states use car registration as a way to check the safety of automobiles. Some states force car owners to have their cars checked once or twice a year. Unless the car meets the state's safety standards, the owner cannot renew the car's registration.

 Every year about 7 million cars end up in junkyards!

166

Why do you need seat belts and shoulder harnesses in a car?

SECURITY IS WHEN THE SEAT BELT CAN STRETCH AROUND YOU AND YOUR BLANKET.

Seat belts and shoulder harnesses keep passengers from being thrown into the windshield, onto the floor, or out of the car during an accident. So seat belts and shoulder harnesses help prevent serious injuries and save lives.

MY MOM AND DAD WERE GOING ON A LITTLE VACATION, BUT THEY CHANGED THEIR MINDS

MOM IS KIND OF A WORRIER

SHE SAYS, WHAT IF THEY WERE DRIVING ALONG THE FREEWAY DOING ABOUT SEVENTY, AND SUDDENLY SOMETHING WENT WRONG WITH THE GLOVE COMPARTMENT?

THAT IS SOMETHING TO WORRY ABOUT

What does a speed limit on a road mean?

Usually a speed limit tells a driver the fastest speed at which it is safe to drive on a certain road. (Occasionally it also tells the slowest speed.) Some roads post only one speed limit. Other roads post different speed limits depending on the weather.

The United States has a national highway speed limit of 55 miles (88 kilometers) an hour. This limit is meant to save gasoline as well as lives. When moving at higher speeds, automobiles waste gasoline.

If a car goes over the speed limit, the driver may be stopped by a policeman and given a speeding ticket. The driver then has to pay a fine. If he gets too many speeding tickets, the state government will take away his driver's license.

TELL YOUR DAD I'LL WASH HIS CAR FOR A DOLLAR

HE WANTS TO KNOW IF YOU HAVE WORKMAN'S COMPENSATION.. WHAT HAPPENS IF YOU'RE INJURED ON THE JOB?

TELL HIM I ONLY WASH CARS THAT ARE STANDING STILL!

There are more automobiles in the state of California than in all of Europe!

167

Why do some racing cars look so strange?

Racing cars are built for speed and power. Many cars, like those in the Grand Prix (grawn pree) races, have sleek bodies. They are built narrow and close to the ground. Most racing cars also have very wide tires. These tires are good for going around corners very fast. They also help give the car power. Some racing cars even have "wings" mounted on their backs. These wings, also called aerofoil (AIR-o-foyl) tails, are not meant to lift the cars off the ground. In fact, they do just the opposite. They help the cars stay down on the road, which makes them go faster.

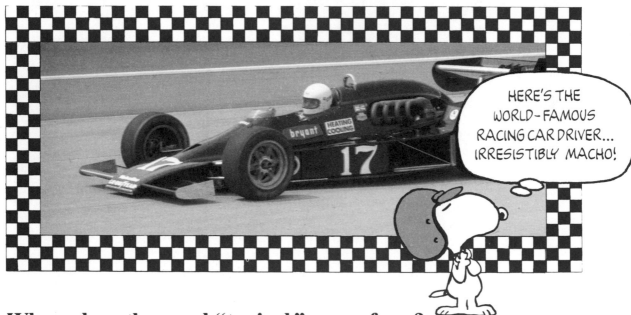

HERE'S THE WORLD-FAMOUS RACING CAR DRIVER... IRRESISTIBLY MACHO!

Where does the word "taxicab" come from?

Although people were hiring carriages and other vehicles for thousands of years, the name "taxicab" wasn't used until the 1800s. The "cab" in "taxicab" is short for "cabriolet" (cab-ree-uh-LAY), a type of one-horse carriage. People hired cabriolets to carry them over short distances. Inside the cabriolet was a taximeter (TACK-see-mee-tur), a machine which kept track of the fare due for the ride. Modern taxicabs have taximeters in them, too. "Taxi" is short for "taximeter."

In October 1929, New York City had 29,000 taxis. That is the largest fleet of taxis that has ever existed in one city!

What kind of car have astronauts used on the moon?

On each of three Apollo moon expeditions, astronauts traveled on the moon's surface in a lunar rover. A rover looks something like a jeep or a dune buggy. But its top and sides are completely open. There is no need to cover the astronaut riders since the moon has no wind and no rain. However, the rover does have fenders. Its moving wheels stir up dust. The fenders keep the dust from blowing in the astronauts' faces. A lunar rover runs on battery power. It has no engine.

What happened to the lunar rovers? All three were left on the moon!

Lunar roving vehicle

Why do we have public transportation?

Years ago most people lived close enough to their jobs to walk to them. But as cities grew, people often had to work farther away from home. They needed a way to get around. Owning a carriage cost too much. So bus and streetcar lines were built. They carried many people at one time and charged only a small fare. More recently, subways and commuter trains have carried many riders, too.

Some people drive their cars to work. But good public transportation is much better than cars in a city. Too many cars dirty the air and cause traffic jams. Buses, trains, and streetcars take up less room than the cars needed to carry the same number of people. They also cause less pollution. City parking is hard to find and expensive for cars. But there are no parking problems for people who take public transportation.

169

Where does the word "bus" come from?

The word "bus" is short for "omnibus," which means for everyone.

What were early buses like?

The first buses were simply large carriages drawn by horses. One of the earliest buses carried people around Paris as long ago as 1662. New York City started bus service in 1829 with its "sociable." The sociable was a carriage with enough room to seat ten people. In the same year, London produced its first omnibus. The omnibus was pulled by three horses side by side. This caused terrible traffic jams. The streets weren't wide enough for the omnibus and other traffic, too. Later omnibuses were made narrower and could be pulled by two horses.

Why was the double-decker bus invented?

The London omnibus was very popular. So many people wanted to ride it that there wasn't room for everyone. Some people used to hold on to the roof. Because of this, a long bus seat was added to the roof of the carriage in 1847. Seats on the open top were half-price. Later, a canopy was added to protect passengers from rain and sun. Today double-decker buses run in cities such as London and New York. But the new ones have closed tops.

What are the longest buses in the world?

The longest buses are each 76 feet (23 meters) long. That's twice as long as an average bus. These very long buses have room enough to seat 121 people. They are used in the Middle East.

San Francisco cable car

What is a streetcar?

A streetcar is any vehicle that moves along rails which are set into the surface of the road. It usually runs within city limits. Early streetcars were pulled by horses. The horses didn't have to work as hard pulling streetcars as they did pulling buses. The rails made their task easier. At the same time, the passengers got a smoother ride.

There are two kinds of streetcars. They get their power, not from horses, but from electricity. One modern streetcar is the trolley car. It gets its power from an overhead electric line. The other modern streetcar is the cable car. It is pulled by a heavy steel rope called a cable. The cable moves along a slot under the surface of the street.

New York State ski gondola

How are cable cars used?

Cable cars are used to climb steep hills and mountains. In San Francisco, the hills are so steep that buses and trolleys have trouble climbing them. So cable cars do the job.

There is a second kind of cable car that is not a streetcar. This kind hangs from steel ropes that are strung between tall towers. As the cables move, the car moves. Such cable cars are often used to take passengers up mountains. You can see these cable cars in many ski areas.

Hanging cable cars carry more than passengers. They also carry things such as tools and supplies.

172

Why do streetcars and trains run on rails?

A vehicle running on rails doesn't hit holes, ruts, mud, or bumps as a car or a wagon on the road does. Also, pulling a car on rails takes less energy, or effort, than pulling a car of the same weight along a road. When a car runs on rails there is less friction, or rubbing, to hold back the wheels. So they roll faster and more freely.

When did people first start using trains?

The very first trains were used by miners before 1600. These trains had no motors and they weren't pulled by animals. They were simple wooden tubs which the miners pushed along wooden rails. Later, miners used horses for pulling wagons along the tracks.

An early train used a "horse engine." The horse ran on an endless belt which was connected to the train's wheels!

Another early train used a sail. The wind moved the train along the rails!

 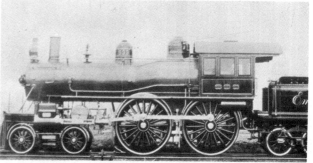

When was the first railroad built?

The first public railroad was built in England in 1825. It ran along 20 miles (32 kilometers) of metal tracks. At first the plan was to have horses pull the trains. But the railroad company decided to use steam engines instead. Each steam engine was able to pull a much heavier load than horses would have been able to pull. Because of this, the railroad was a great success. Five years later an even bigger railroad was built in England.

How fast were the first railroad trains?

In 1830 a steam locomotive named "Rocket" reached a speed of 29 miles (46 kilometers) an hour. People thought that was very fast. And it *was* for that time—for the average train moved at about 15 miles (24 kilometers) an hour.

Laid end to end, the tracks of the world's main railroad routes would stretch 750,000 miles (1,200,000 kilometers). That's almost three times the distance between the earth and the moon!

How fast are modern trains?

The average modern train travels at about 65 miles (104 kilometers) an hour. However, some trains today average more than 100 miles (160 kilometers) an hour.

What is a locomotive?

A locomotive is the railroad car that holds the train's engine. Most locomotives are at the front of a train and pull it. But some are at the back of a train and push it, instead. People sometimes use the word "locomotive" to mean the engine itself.

How do modern trains run?

Most modern trains are pulled by locomotives that use diesel-electric engines. A diesel-electric engine is similar to a gasoline engine. But it burns oil instead of gasoline. The oil-burning diesel turns generators. These generators supply electrical energy to turn the locomotive's wheels.

Some locomotives are fully electric. They use no oil. They get electric current from wires hung above the railroad track or from a third rail that runs on the ground inside the track. As in the diesel engine, the electric power turns the train wheels.

Do American railroads make most of their money from passengers?

No. In the United States about $95.00 out of every $100.00 that railroads earn comes from carrying freight. Freight includes packages, metals, animals, and lumber. In the United States as many as ten thousand freight trains are on the move every day. In Europe, however, passenger trains are quite popular.

What's the longest freight train on record?

The longest freight train stretched 4 miles (more than 6 kilometers). It was made up of 500 coal cars and 6 diesel locomotives—3 at the front and 3 at about the middle of the train. This freight train traveled 157 miles (251 kilometers) on the Norfolk and Western Railway on November 15, 1967. The train weighed 47,000 tons (42,300 metric tons). An average freight train has about 100 cars.

Why are freight trains so long?

One reason is that many railroads are being asked to carry more freight than ever before. A second reason is that different kinds of freight cars are needed to carry different kinds of freight.

For example, boxcars carry grains, cans, and packages. Boxcars are completely enclosed. Flatcars are open platforms used for carrying logs, steel, machinery, and even automobiles. Stock cars carry cattle, pigs, or sheep. And tank cars hold liquids, such as oil. There are also refrigerator cars, poultry cars, and milk cars—to name a few.

The Trans-Siberian Railroad in the U.S.S.R. is so long that it would stretch from New York to California and back again!

John Massis moved two cars of a train
by pulling them with his teeth.
The cars weighed 80 tons
(72 metric tons)!

ANYWAY...
MOST OF THE CREDIT SHOULD
GO TO HIS MOTHER WHO
PROBABLY MADE HIM BRUSH
AFTER EVERY MEAL
—RIGHT SIR?...

Why are railroad tunnels built?

Most railroad tunnels are built through the rock of hills and mountains. Instead of winding miles and miles of tracks around a mountain, builders prefer to cut through the mountain in a straight line. Then the train route is shorter—and safer, too!

How is a railroad tunnel built?

Workers drill holes deep into the side of a hill or a mountain. They pack explosives such as dynamite into the holes. Huge sections of rock and earth are blasted away in seconds. The workers clear away the loose rock and drill more holes. After they have cleared the tunnel all the way through, they line it with concrete. Then they lay down tracks. Now the railroad tunnel is ready to be used.

What do train whistles mean?

Locomotive engineers use train whistles to signal to crew members and other railroad workers. Whistles also warn people and animals that a train is coming. "Whistle talk" is a code made up of short and long toots. For example, one short toot means "Apply brakes. Stop." Two long toots are a signal to release the train's brakes and start moving.

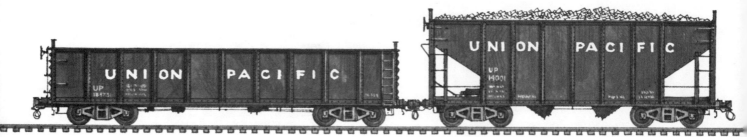

How do railroads prevent accidents?

Railroads have many ways of preventing accidents besides train-whistle warnings. One of these is the block signal system. A block is a length of railroad track, usually one or two miles long. To prevent collisions, only one train at a time is allowed in a block. Colored lights signal whether a train may enter a block. Red means stop. Green means go. And yellow means go ahead with caution. When one train is already in a block, the signals warn other trains to stop. Some block signals are hand-operated. Railroad people along the line control those signals. Other block signals work automatically.

Some locomotives have special panels on which signals give the same information as the signal lights on the tracks. If an engineer does not notice a panel signal to stop, the train will stop automatically. Finally, crew members use two-way radios to speak with faraway stations and train yards.

179

What's the largest railroad station in the world?

The world's largest railroad station is Grand Central Terminal in New York City. It has two floors and covers 48 acres (about 19 hectares). That's about the size of 37 football fields. There are 67 tracks running into the station. On an average day about 550 trains and more than 180,000 people use this station.

What is a monorail?

A monorail is a railroad that has only one rail. Most railroads have two. This rail may be above or below the monorail cars. Monorail cars are often powered by gasoline engines or electric motors. Monorails are faster and cheaper to run than two-rail lines.

What is a subway?

A subway is a passenger railroad that runs mostly underground. It gets its power from electricity. Because it is underground, a subway is perfect for a crowded city. Except for its station entrances, it does not take up any street space. Since subways carry people all around a city, they must make many stops along their routes.

When was the first city subway opened?

The first subway was opened in London, England, on January 10, 1863. The trains used steam locomotives that burned coke (later coal). It was nicknamed "the sewer," for it smelled horrible, and was terribly dirty and dark. Some passengers carried candles to light their way. Pickpockets were always at work. Nonetheless, this first subway carried nearly 10 million passengers in its first year.

Which is the busiest subway system in the world?

The busiest subway system in the world belongs to New York City. In 1970, New York's subways carried more than 2 billion passengers. By 1976, the number had gone down to about 1 billion 27 million. But so far, New York's subways are still the busiest.

How many cities in the world have subways?

There are 67 subways in the world today. Besides New York, some of the cities with large subway systems are Paris, London, Berlin, Moscow, Hamburg, Tokyo, and Boston. Not all cities call them "subways," however. Some have the name "metro" and others "underground."

The Tokyo, Japan, subway system hires special workers to squeeze passengers into crowded trains!

What will trains of the future be like?

Some future trains will have no wheels! Instead they may be lifted above the tracks by an air cushion or by magnets. Such trains would be very quiet. And they would not wear out quickly because they would not rub against the tracks. Magnetic trains are already being tested.

Trains of an even more distant future may run by gravity—the force which pulls everything on earth toward its center. The trains would move through a long airless tunnel. Both ends of the tunnel would slant steeply toward the center. The train would run downhill to the middle of the tunnel. By then it would be moving at a speed of many thousands of miles an hour. This is so fast that the train would be able to travel to the other end of the tunnel before slowing to a stop.

Twin tank truck

Why are there many different kinds of trucks?

Many different kinds of trucks are needed to do many different kinds of jobs. Refrigerator trucks carry food that would spoil if it were not kept cold. Tank trucks carry liquids such as gasoline. Dump trucks tilt so they can unload things easily. Tractors and trailers carry huge loads over long distances. Small enclosed trucks called panel trucks carry small loads over short distances. Vans are long trucks that move furniture. And bottle trucks have special racks for holding cases of bottles.

These are only a few examples of the many kinds of trucks. More than 600 companies in the United States build thousands of special kinds of trucks. Today there are more than 12 million trucks in the United States.

Motor vehicle transporter

Flat-bed trailer

What is a trailer?

A trailer is a van or wagon that is pulled by another vehicle. It has no engine of its own. One kind of trailer, called a mobile home, can be pulled by a car or a truck. It is outfitted with beds, seats, and even a bathroom and a kitchen. Many people spend their vacations traveling around in trailers. Other people live in them all the time.

Another kind of trailer carries freight. It is so big that it must be pulled by a powerful tractor truck.

Three-wheel truck

The first postal trucks in the United States were made so that a mule could be hitched to one if the steam engine failed to work!

What is a tractor truck?

A tractor truck is the front part of a big tractor-trailer, or "rig." It contains the engine and the cab, where the driver sits. The tractor truck can be driven without the trailer, but the trailer can't be driven without the tractor. The trailer has no engine of its own. Power for the trailer's brakes and lights comes from the tractor truck.

Dump truck

Cement truck

KEEP ON TRUCKIN'!! HA HA HA HA HA

In 1904 there were only 700 trucks being used in the United States. Fourteen years later the number had gone up to 250,000!

What were the first fire trucks like?

The first fire trucks were simply water pumps on wheels that men pulled to fires. Europeans used those simple hand trucks in the 1500s.

In the early 1800s, American fire companies used steam pumps, or engines, pulled by men or horses. Fire companies tried to outdo each other by hiring artists to paint beautiful scenes on the sides of their engines. They gave the engines fancy names such as "Live Oak" and "Ocean Wave."

Fire horses of the early 1900s were well trained.
As soon as the fire alarm rang, the horses trotted out
from their stalls by themselves and
stood ready in front of the fire trucks!

What were the first ambulances like?

The first ambulances were probably horse-drawn carts. The Spanish army used them to carry its wounded off the battlefield in 1487. Before that armies probably used litters and stretchers to carry wounded soldiers.

187

How do people travel across snow?

Wheels sink into snow. So people have invented ways of gliding over it. People have made snowshoes and skis. They have also made vehicles with runners such as sleds, sleighs, and snowmobiles.

What are snowshoes?

Snowshoes are made of light, wooden frames that have strings of leather stretched across them. They look something like long oval tennis rackets. They have straps that fasten to a person's boots. Someone wearing snowshoes can walk on deep snow without sinking into it. Snowshoes work because they spread a person's weight over a large area.

American Indians invented snowshoes. Today people wear them while hunting, farming, taking care of forests, or just for fun. People who wear snowshoes usually use ski poles or special ice picks to help them keep their balance.

When did people start using skis?

People have used skis for more than 5,000 years. Skiing began as a way of getting around in places where there was a lot of snow. The first skis were probably made from animal bones.

188

What is cross-country skiing?

When you go cross-country skiing, you don't just go down hills. You may ski uphill, downhill, or on flat land. Cross-country skiers usually ski long distances, often on country trails. Their skis are narrower and lighter than downhill skis.

What are sleds and sleighs?

A sled is a vehicle on runners. People use sleds for much more than playing in the snow. Until snowmobiles were invented, sleds pulled by dogs were the only vehicles that could move people and things over the ice and the snow.

A sleigh is a kind of sled with curved runners. Its seat is a foot or more above the ground. Horse-drawn sleighs were very popular before people had automobiles with snow tires.

What are snowmobiles?

Snowmobiles are sleds with motors. Instead of long runners, snowmobiles have two short skis in front. The rider steers the skis with handlebars. At the back is a wide belt made for gripping the snow.

Most snowmobiles can speed along at 50 miles (80 kilometers) an hour. Some can go faster than 100 miles (160 kilometers) an hour. In some snowy places, snowmobiles are the only fast way to get around. So they are important to ski patrols, doctors, and the police. Today, Eskimos usually use snowmobiles instead of dog sleds. And many people ride them and race them just for fun.

Snowmobile race

What is a toboggan?

A toboggan is a vehicle without runners that glides on snow and ice. A toboggan is made of long strips of wood that curl up at the front. The underside of a toboggan is highly polished. So it glides easily and moves very fast.

American Indians made the first toboggans to carry things across snow. Today, people still use toboggans to carry things. But they are more popular as vehicles for sport. People coast down hills in toboggans or down special long, straight trails.

192

Did You Know That...

Big 18-wheel tractor-trailers usually zoom along superhighways. But the truck trailers can also ride "piggy-back" aboard railroad flatcars. Traveling this way, the trailers can go long distances without tying up the highways or using gasoline.

A special passenger train carries automobiles between Virginia and Florida. When the passengers reach their destination, they claim their cars and drive away.

Tractor-trailer being put on flatcar

Escalators are moving stairways. They carry large crowds of people between floors in stores, shopping malls, and subway stations. The first demonstration of an escalator was in Paris in 1900. Escalators today can carry more than 6,000 people every hour.

PSYCHIATRIC HELP 25¢

THE DOCTOR IS IN

THAT'S YOUR TROUBLE, CHARLIE BROWN. YOU'RE ALWAYS TRYING TO GO DOWN THE UP ESCALATOR!

Bulldozers or earth movers run on continuous metal tracks instead of wheels. The tracks spread the weight of the bulldozer over a greater area and keep the machine from sinking into soft ground. And because the tracks are rigid, the bulldozers can ride over rough surfaces easily.

Bulldozer

The first elevator with a safety brake was invented in 1853. The early elevators were powered by steam engines or pressure from water or oil. Today most elevators are run by electricity. Because of elevators, people can live and work in tall buildings. Some elevators with glass walls travel on the outside of buildings. Passengers get a view with their ride. The swiftest elevators can go faster than 20 miles an hour!

Some sidewalks move. They are really belts of rubber that carry people along flat surfaces or up slight slopes. These sidewalks help the flow of crowds through long airport or museum corridors. And it sure beats walking.

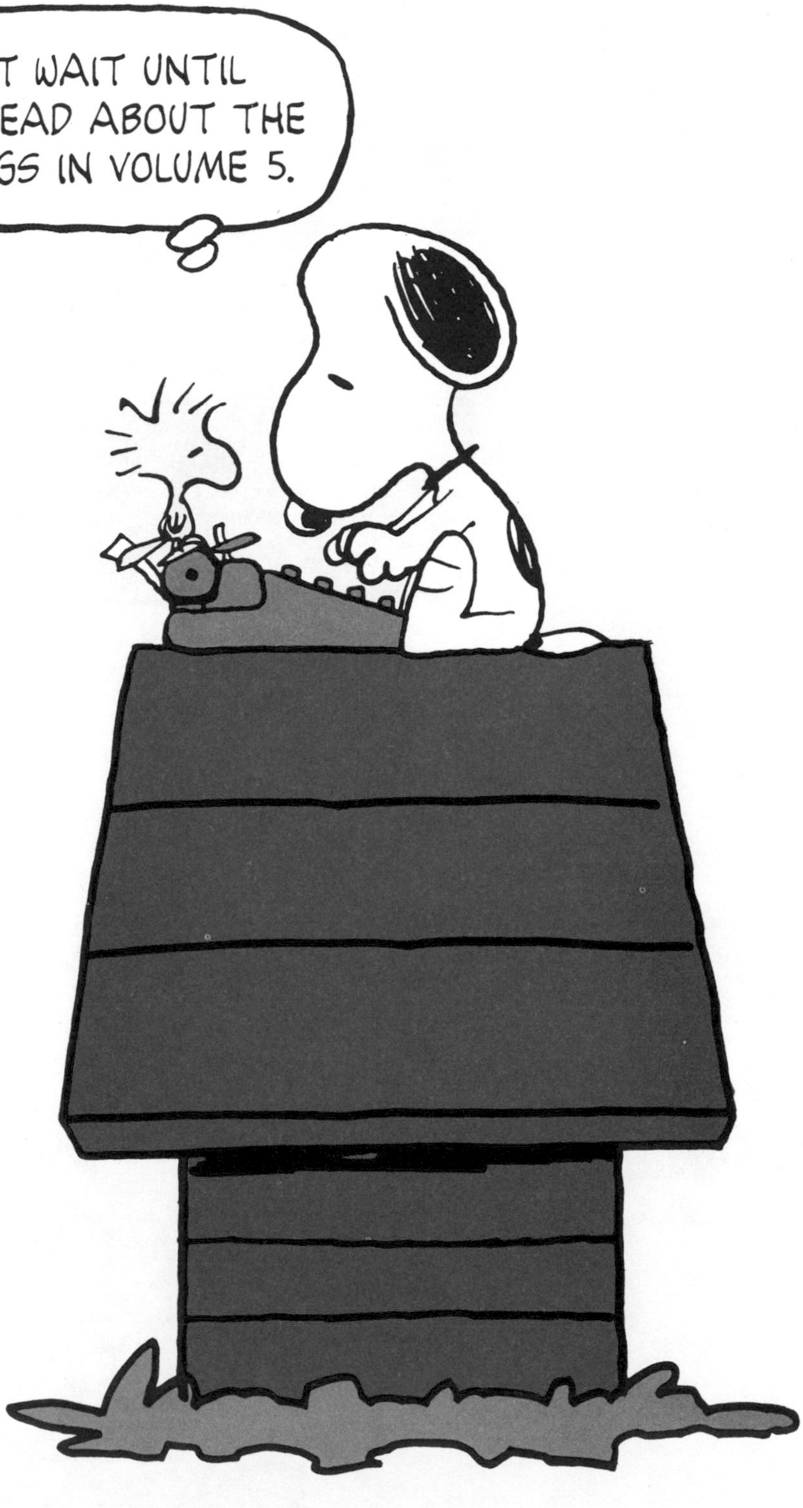
BUT WAIT UNTIL YOU READ ABOUT THE VIKINGS IN VOLUME 5.